WITHDRAWN

Planning to Learn

Planning to Learn

Creating and Using a Personal Planner
with Young People on the Autism Spectrum

Keely Harper-Hill and Stephanie Lord

Jessica Kingsley Publishers
London and Philadelphia

First published in 2007
by Jessica Kingsley Publishers
116 Pentonville Road
London N1 9JB, UK
and
400 Market Street, Suite 400
Philadelphia, PA 19106, USA

www.jkp.com

Library of Congress Cataloging in Publication Data

Harper-Hill, Keely.

Planning to learn : creating and using a personal planner with young people on the autism spectrum / Keely Harper-Hill and Stephanie Lord.

p. cm.

ISBN-13: 978-1-84310-561-9 (pb : alk. paper) 1. Autistic children--Rehabilitation. 2. Autism in adolescence. I. Lord, Stephanie. II. Title.

RJ506.A9H2684 2007

618.92'85882--dc22

2007014660

British Library Cataloguing in Publication Data
A CIP catalogue record for this book is available from the British Library

ISBN 978 1 84310 561 9

Printed and bound in Great Britain by
Printwise (Haverhill) Ltd, Suffolk

Contents

Introduction

Learning from experience

The ideas in this planner are from our direct work with children and young people over the years. Many of these students had received a late diagnosis of autism spectrum conditions.

Late diagnosis means late interventions, which for these young people often meant that they had failed to learn strategies to help them on a daily basis. They learnt survival strategies that were not necessarily appropriate or long term. Parents and practitioners became confused because the young people appeared to be in control of their learning, but in reality were struggling to understand their world. The young people frequently found their education made no connection to their thinking process and they found it hard to carry knowledge from one context to another. They often appeared to act on impulse without thinking; or seemed disorganised, failing to learn from direct or past experiences, repeating the same patterns of unsuccessful behaviour over and over again.

Disorganised thinkers need help with shaping life skills into a kit that they can carry around with them. This is why the planner is important.

We will start by giving you two examples. John enjoyed Maths lessons, but became upset if Maths was cancelled and he had an unexpected lesson. Before he had a planner, a change of plan such as English instead of Maths would mean he would experience meltdown and would need to be taken out of the class for the whole morning.

John's teacher has now put together a personal planner for him using the exercises in this book. The planner is an A5 ringbinder containing:

- a daily timetable including lessons, break times, mealtimes and evening activities

- a pocket with cards to remind him of strategies such as 'think it, don't say it' and 'breathe and blow' to help him breathe deeply to calm down

- a list of jobs divided into Easy, Hard, Fun and Never tried

- pages from planning sessions for him to refer back to.

Now when Maths is cancelled John's teacher puts a yellow sticky note on his daily timetable so that he knows there will be a change. If he is introducing a new activity that he knows John won't like, he will suggest John does one of his 'fun jobs' afterwards. John has a list of fun jobs in his planner that he can choose from.

Vincent is another young person. When we met him he was 12 years old. Vincent spoke well and he was perceived as articulate and organised. This meant that when he couldn't cope with classroom situations, Vincent was considered to be choosing to behave in a way which was challenging. When he was worried or scared, Vincent behaved in such a way that he was permitted to leave the class – with no demands placed on him. This developed as his strategy for dealing with difficult situations – he would leave the situation 'in anger' and walk around the grounds. He had no strategies for talking or thinking about the situation.

Observations of Vincent revealed that he became anxious when the adult he was expecting to work with was absent. He often did not understand what was said when people spoke too fast or when he was upset. He became very worried when he had to interact with more than one person. When Vincent became worried, scared or angry, he also became scared by the way his heart beat faster and he wasn't able to breathe.

Working with an adult, Vincent adapted a regular filofax as his planner. The planner was black, small and inconspicuous. These were things which were very important to Vincent as he wanted to be able to keep the planner in his pocket. In this planner he carried:

- a visual reminder to breathe deeply ('breathe and blow') – although he wrote and drew his own picture

- a weekly and daily timetable so that he understood what tasks he was expected to complete, and which adults would be available to help him

- communication cards that allowed him to communicate non-verbally at times of stress; for example, 'You are making too much noise!', 'I need time to think – back in five minutes'

- sheets requesting 'debriefs' with adults so that he could organise a time to talk and think about an experience that had ended badly.

This means that Vincent is able to calm himself and stay in control. He is able to choose more appropriate actions instead of the aimless walking that he used when we first met him. Adults working with him can also prompt him: 'Your breathing looks fast – is there anything you need to do?' When he becomes confused, Vincent can look at his timetable to remind himself what he has to do. The timetable can be used by adults who work with Vincent so that any changes to his routine are shown visually. The use of communication cards means that Vincent is able to communicate with those around him when he is worried, scared or anxious. The nature of these cards can help other people to change the way they talk to Vincent – which is great when this is what is making him worried. Vincent is beginning to understand that adults can be helpful to sort out problems.

Vincent is due to begin work experience. He will take his planner with him as all of these strategies will be needed there.

Before you begin:

- read the rest of the introduction

- follow the instructions to make your own kit, and

- set up a basic planner.

It is important that you read and understand each topic before you start work. You will find a list of the five key concepts covered at the start of each topic. The topics in this book have been divided into sessions so that the young person can tackle one piece of thinking at a time. Notes for your role as 'the shaper' are included at the beginning of each session. You may choose to copy the worksheets to save the young person having to write directly in this book.

Each session should take between 30 minutes and an hour. The young person will need to carry the lessons learnt into everyday life. At the end of each session any useful cards and worksheets should be added to the planner so that the young person has them to hand when they need them.

Keep your kit with you and you will always be ready to build on the work you are doing in the sessions, or use a card or mantra to help the young person to carry out the plan they have made.

Practical planning

The practical ideas we are going to introduce directly address the difficulties in attention, memory, coping and calming skills. We will call your role as the supporting adult, 'the shaper'. As you learn about planning and start to use the planner consistently, you will be building up a resource that will support the young person as they move into adulthood.

We want you to remember that each young person is a uniquely different thinker, so sometimes the text we provide will need to be adapted.

You can do this by using:

- a thought bubble

- a speech bubble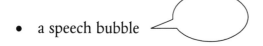

- or an adhesive note to indicate '*Here's another way you can try to do this*'.

We developed the mantra 'You can make a plan'. It's what we say to the young person. It can become your mantra too. Mantras are set phrases that we use to help the person understand what we mean – by saying the same words every time. Whenever a difficulty arises, whenever there has been an incident – we want to make a plan with the young person. Initially for your own confidence you need to practise the basic skills with the mantra 'Let's make a plan'.

Sometimes we make things worse by what we say. You will have your own personal mantra:

Think it, don't say it; write it down!

This means that you stop yourself from adding to the noise that the young person will have to process and understand. Instead you write what you want to say to the young person.

When you are making a plan you can agree with the young person what you will say to try to help them. This needs to be simple and short. At times of difficulty it will be all you say. For example:

You *think* everything else but you only *say* the mantra. It might be that you don't say anything and write down the mantra. You can talk about this when you are making a plan:

Don't forget the good times.

It is really easy to focus on using set mantras only when a young person's behaviour is challenging. But they are also a good way to promote understanding in many situations, so make sure you have stock phrases to let the young person know...

Making your kit

Before you start making a planner with the young person, you need to set up a kit for yourself. This kit will help you to assist them to become organised. By using your own kit you will be modelling and shaping the positive habits you want the young person to develop.

It might help to think of this kit as your own box of tools that will help you to help the young person in their learning.

It's about thinking, recording and organising the daily activities or events that occur within the home setting, place of learning or place of work. As the shaper you are going to help the young person understand how typical (but organised) people get themselves through their day. You will show how making a plan helps you to get through the day without being overwhelmed by anxiety. Your kit will hold all of the tools you will need to do this.

Your basic kit includes:

- Photocopies or line drawings of the strategies and plans they are learning to use. These things need to be handy – you'll get used to carrying them at all times either in a shoulder bag or deep pocket. You will use the graphics or cards as visual prompts to encourage the young person to use a plan that you have made together. Each topic includes strategies and plans that will be useful to photocopy.

- Paper, card, adhesive notes, pens, pencils, highlighter, masking tape, paperclips, blu tack…

- Tangible rewards – these are items that you can give as an instant reward to motivate, hold attention and increase self-belief. When the person is trying hard and has finished a difficult job, you give them a reward. Think beyond sweets or goodies – what is the person into? A picture of a tractor, a bus ticket, a cash till tape… Get a range of possible items that the person may find interesting – show them that you are putting them in your kit and see what grabs their attention.

Making the planner

The planner refers to the filofax or organiser that the young person will carry with them. This will hold the key plans for the young person and so is central to the notion of them becoming in charge of their learning.

You may want to involve the young person in every stage of making the planner, or in some cases you might find it easier to set up a basic planner first and then work with the young person to customise it as you go along.

What you need for a basic planner

- An A4 or A5 ringbinder

- Section dividers labelled: Making a Plan; Plans to Calm; Plans to Be Organised; Plans to Be with People; Plans to Think

- Some blank paper for writing on

- A plastic file pocket to keep picture cards in

- Spare section dividers so you can add important information.

The shaper needs to keep thinking about what goes into the planner. What you write or draw needs to help the young person to arrange their thoughts into a workable sequence or routine so they can:

- make sense of the task

- focus on organisation

- be less worried by having a plan.

As the shaper, it is important that you are clear about how the young person will make sense of the way the information is organised. Read through the guidance sections on your own. Have more than one planner that the young person can choose – it may be that you offer a choice of a small filofax with adapted sections, but then also an A4 ringbinder file. Once the young person has chosen what they consider to be acceptable you can work through the sections together. As you complete each section and make a plan, this can then be put into the relevant section of the young person's planner. Sometimes the plan you have made will be photo-copied sheets from the workbook. Other times, when you have really individualised a strategy it will be truly unique – all of these are valid plans to have made. What is important is that they work for the young person.

Remember that you may not be the adult who is there when the young person next needs help, so it is a good idea if the planner also makes sense to anyone else who needs to look at it.

Making it a habit

To get into the habit of planning regularly, you need to think about where you will work with the young person. This space works best if it:

- has a table and chairs

- is clear and tidy

- provides peace and quiet with no distractions.

not too cluttered   not too comfortable

A kit means you will have everything you need to do the job, ready and prepared. This job may be to assist in planning the day or it may be to help the young person think about something that has happened.

Experience has taught us that if we don't have our kit with us all the time we become

the talker

instead of

the shaper

blah blah blah

I don't want that to happen again. Next time I will write it down.

If you need to, practise drawing your think and speech bubbles:

 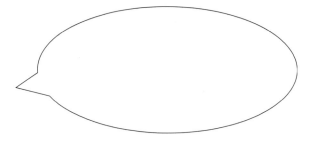

Or a stick man:

The person in this planner wasn't drawn by an artist – so have a go, you might suprise yourself. It takes practice (and a sense of humour).

Using video to practise planning and learning

You must get permission to video the person from the parent or legal guardian.

The process of making a plan is very important for young people. It provides the opportunity to reflect upon why they need to plan some activities and to plan their responses to particular events. The young person's ability to know what they should be doing can be more insightful than their behaviour suggests. The planner is an active process of learning new skills: new ways of thinking and new ways of doing. You will need to teach the young person what to do.

In our experience we have found the most positive outcomes have come from the following sequence of activities:

1. Make the plan.

2. Practise what you have planned. Follow the plan you've made with a simple game.

3. Role-play the plan together and video this:

   • First define the activity as pretend. Check that the young person knows what pretend means (not real/playing/practising). Using a video camera can help to reinforce that it is pretend.

   • Simulate the scenario – be as realistic as you can.

   • Use the visual supports, e.g. a card showing 'breathe and blow'.

   • After each role-play, begin with feedback to remind the young person that it was only pretend – 'Good pretending – that looked real!'

   • Then ask the young person to think about what they felt inside – what their body felt like; maybe what their breathing was like.

   • Playback the video.

   • Give explicit, positive feedback – 'I really liked the way you…' (e.g. looked at your visual, tried to breathe and blow; stood so still…).

   • Ask the young person to say the things they did that they thought were good.

   • You may find many things that could be done differently. Talk about them, and choose *one* to work on.

   • Explain why this could be done differently and you'll find examples of this in Topic 4, Plans to Be with People.

- Practise this small change and then:

- Role-play again!

4. Use real-life opportunities to put the plans into place.

Think about the everyday activities and interactions that the young person is to be involved in. For example, you may have made a plan to use 'breathe and blow' from Topic 2 Plans to Calm to cope with change. You are just about to inform the young person of a change. You would begin by having the young person look up and check what their plan for change is. Then you could inform the young person of the change and prompt them to use their plan.

It is important to actively look for opportunities for the young person to practise their plans.

Sharing good practice

Where you have used a visual card or a mantra to facilitate learning, share your successes by letting other adults know what these are.

Topic 1: Making a Plan

Session 1.1: Introducing the plan
Session 1.2: Easy job or hard job?

The **five key concepts** to communicate in these sessions:

1. Organised people make a plan.

2. You get organised by making a plan.

3. When things don't go according to plan your body feels like…

4. Think 'breathe and blow' to stay calm when the plan goes wrong.

5. We all have jobs to do.

Session 1.1: Introducing the plan – notes for shapers

In this session

This first session sets the scene for the young person as to the nature of the project ahead – to begin to use a planner.

The notion of naming body sensations, how it feels when things go wrong, is introduced. Think of incidents that the young person has been involved in so you will have examples that you can use to aid their understanding, 'Remember when you had that supply teacher? She talked and talked. You just had enough. It was hard.' A word of caution: choose your examples carefully. You want to help the student see the relevance of making a plan. You don't necessarily want to relive a particularly negative experience.

Then on page 26 we introduce the use of mantras, these are words that help. If you have gained permission to use video you might want to introduce it as part of making a plan. Young people can sometimes find this idea challenging. Persevere – let them see you being videoed. It is worth it.

Before you begin

Read and photocopy the worksheets on pages 22–28, or have the young person write directly in this book.

Have your kit ready (see p.12).

During the session

Work through pages 22–28.

You will need to think about your own strategies for being organised. You will need to show and share these ideas.

Identify two situations that the student has previously found difficult so you can prompt their recall and support their thinking.

You will need to help the young person draw where they experienced different sensations in their body. This is on pages 23 and 24. You can model this by drawing your own feelings. Get the young person to think about how different their body feels when they are calm, from when they are scared, worried or angry. Once you have finished, these pages can be put into the planner. As the planner becomes filled with other plans, you may choose to remove these pages.

Using the planner

Keep the strategies covered in the planner, so that students are able to refer to plans such as 'breathe and blow' whenever they feel stressed. Other adults working with them will be able to look at their plans to see what will help the young person.

What are plans for?

This book is called *A Planner*. Planners help people get organised.

Read this section: with an adult   ☐   ☑
                     by yourself.   ☐

Lots of people find their day goes easier if they have made a plan.

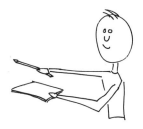

They may use a diary, or make a list, but they always write down their daily jobs.

Organised people use a planner.

Most people find some things hard. They get worried, scared and even angry. When things go wrong it can be horrible. It can make you worry that it will happen again.

Do you get worried, scared or angry?

What is it like when things go wrong?

🖉 Show *where* you feel it…

Maybe you feel a certain colour?

🖉 Show what colour you feel…

What word would you use to describe this feeling?

🖉 how you feel…

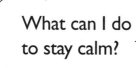

Worried ☐   Scared ☐   Angry ☐

This is the time to use a plan!

Making a plan can help you think…

What can I do to stay calm?

What could I try next time?

What can I do when I don't know what's happening?

23

What is it like inside you when…

✎ You are calm?

✎ You don't know what is happening?

You can choose:

☑ to stay calm

☑ to find out what's going on

☑ to ask for help

☑ to do good thinking

Planning puts you in control – you can choose to:

☑ take some time to chill out

☑ check out what you are supposed to do

☑ ask for help

One of the good things about making a plan is...

I can write it down.

If you get really angry or stressed and you can't talk, you can plan to...

✏ write it down

and then show it to someone who can help:

☑ Mum

☑ Dad

☑ grandparents

☑ teacher

☑ helper

☑ supervisor

☑ other person

Words that help

Sometimes, people *have* to talk to help you. Something you can try to do is agree on set things they can say. So if someone has agreed to help you to breathe and blow, that's all they say:

Breathe and blow

They might show you the picture to help you.
They might breathe and blow, but they will only say:

Breathe and blow

When you are making plans with an adult maybe you can think about short sentences that they can say that will help you when things get hard.

It might be that all they say is:

Remember, job now,
PlayStation later.

Nothing more, nothing less. It gives you the information you need to make a good choice.

Once you have made a plan, it might mean that you have to learn to:

☑ do something in a new way

☑ do something you have never done before

Read the next page to think about learning, watching and practising something new.

Learning, watching and practising something new

Most times when people learn to do something new, they need some help. When someone asks if you need help, it can be hard to say 'yes'. It can be hard because you may wish that you didn't need help. It can be hard because maybe you don't want anyone else to see that you need help.

Feeling worried about needing help doesn't always make sense. Think about this example:

When you learn to drive, you won't just sit in the car and drive off on your own. This would be madness. It could be dangerous – to you or to other people. You might not even get the car started! If you did start the car, would you know how to change gears or work an automatic? Probably not. But, think about it. You probably wouldn't get out of the car and say:

'It's just an example...'

Driving cars is stupid – it doesn't work.

Driving cars is stupid – I can't do it.

Driving cars is stupid – I'm not doing that again.

You might think:

That is harder than it looks!

I might need someone to help me.

This will take a lot of practice!

Thinking these things will also help you to learn to use the plans you make in this book.

When you make a plan, it can help to try to think:

Who can help me with this?

You would have someone help you in driving lessons. This person would be the driving instructor. You might have someone to help you practise on other roads and at different times. This may be a parent or a family friend.

When you are practising the plans for your planner, you will need someone like the driving instructor. Usually this person is an adult you trust. This adult can help you to:

☑ think about your plans

☑ practise your plans

☑ know how you are succeeding with your plans

This adult will practise with you. This is pretending and you will call it role-play.

This adult will show you how well you are doing. This is by videoing you. At first it can feel strange to be videoed. Videoing is a good way of seeing and thinking about what you are doing.

This adult will help you to practise in real life. They will show or say things to help you use your plans when you are out and about. This is real-world practice. This is what Planning to Learn is all about.

Session 1.2: Easy job or hard job? – notes for shapers

In this session

We provide a framework for helping the young person think about different tasks. The underpinning premise is that we all have to do jobs. Some jobs are okay and others are hard. You may wish to split the okay jobs further depending on the ability of the student. Okay jobs can be described as easy or fun. Hard jobs can be split into 'jobs I don't like, but have to do' and 'jobs I have never tried before'.

'Jobs I have never tried before' may start as hard jobs because of the anxiety they may provoke, but once they've been tried they might be reassigned as easy or fun jobs!

Before you begin

Read and photocopy the worksheets on pages 31–33, or have the young person write directly in this book.

Alternatively, prepare some flipchart paper divided into four columns headed:

Easy jobs, Hard jobs, Fun jobs, Never tried jobs.

During the session

Work through pages 31–33.

Work with the student to list all known activities under the headings of okay/hard. Never tried jobs can be listed under hard, giving an instant rating to such jobs.

For the young person who finds it difficult to complete many tasks that are introduced by an adult, you now have a framework to plan the day's activities. Begin by showing a cycle for the session or day, which may look like this:

1. easy job

2. easy job

3. hard job

4. fun job.

Good thinking. In our school, we do jobs in this order.

This is a cycle that *the adult* has decided. The idea is that if you try something hard then you need to know that something fun will happen afterwards. Something fun can include five minutes reading a book (if that is in the person's list of fun jobs). It doesn't mean a trip to the local theme park. As the shaper you need to help prepare the list of easy/hard jobs in a work order to fit the situation, e.g. at home or at school.

An example could be:

Easy jobs

- Take lunch order to canteen

- Wipe tables

- Complete maths worksheet

- Water plants.

You can choose one of these easy jobs.

In a mainstream environment, with a student who is accessing regular classes there may be particular tasks and jobs that are stressful and belong on the hard list. This type of thinking and planning means that the teacher or aide is in a position to suggest…

I can see this is a hard job. Do the hard job then choose an okay job.

Using the planner

The easy and fun jobs will be listed in the planner and the person can be directed to look and choose so they know what they will do when the hard job is finished. And of course, it would really help to have it written or drawn on an adhesive note and put next to the young person.

1. Complete 5 maths problems

2. 10 minutes reading

Easy job or hard job?

Something to think about:

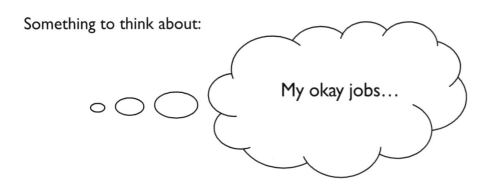

My okay jobs…

Okay jobs are those jobs that are easy or fun for you.

✏ write your okay jobs here

Easy jobs	Fun jobs

If you want these in your planner, write them on page 116.

When you are making your daily plans there will be jobs and tasks that you really like doing. There will also be jobs and tasks that you don't want to do. Jobs and tasks might be given to you by your Mum, Dad, grandparent, teacher or supervisor.

Who else gives you jobs?

 ....

Doing jobs that are *not* on the okay list happens for everyone.

The adults in your life can help you remember this by saying:

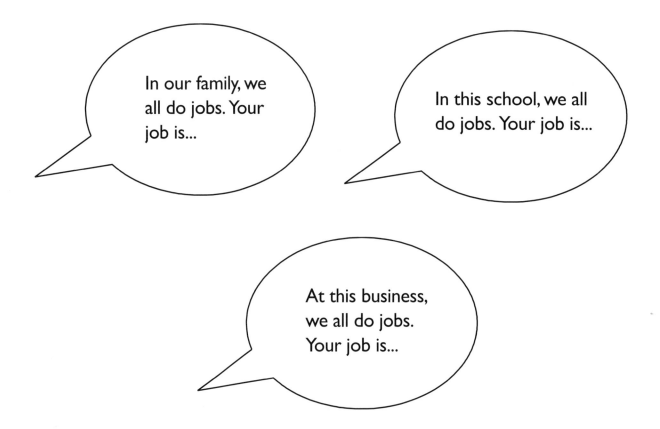

In our family, we all do jobs. Your job is...

In this school, we all do jobs. Your job is...

At this business, we all do jobs. Your job is...

(You might not like hearing this but it is true.)

If you find a job really hard you might want to put it in a list of hard jobs. This can also be a good place to put jobs that you have never tried before. Sometimes when you try a new job, you might want to change it from being a hard job to an easy or fun job.

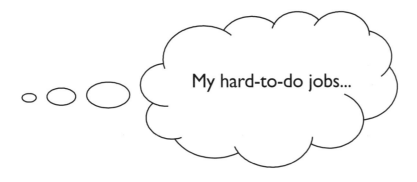

My hard-to-do jobs...

✎ write hard jobs here

Jobs I don't like doing (but have to)	Jobs I have never tried

Remember

Planning a time to do jobs that *have* to be done (some okay and some hard) means:

☑ You can tick off when you are finished.

☑ You ask adults to help you make time for the activities that you like.

☑ You will know when the fun stuff will happen.

Topic 2: Plans to Calm

Session 2.1: Plans to breathe and blow
Session 2.2: Plans to use gesture
Session 2.3: Plans to chill out
Session 2.4: Plans to wait

The **five key concepts** to communicate in these sessions:

1. You can choose to stay calm.

2. Breathing out is calming.

3. Gestures help the brain think because they prompt reflex actions to calm the body.

4. Tell an adult when you need a break.

5. Having a drink or a snack helps with calming.

Session 2.1: Plans to breathe and blow – notes for shapers

In this session

The 'breathe and blow' strategy has been hugely successful with many young people. It is used to regain a sense of calm and control when things have gone wrong. Good thinking cannot happen whilst someone is breathing fast but with practice they learn to remain calm.

The young person needs help to think about what their body feels like when they are losing control. They may feel as if they have just run a race with their heart beating, head dizzy, feeling thirsty. These feelings make you respond differently.

We know about the internal fight, flight and fear responses that result from adrenaline pumping in our bodies, but there is another response that we have observed, the flock response. The flock response refers to when a person is drawn to others and attempts to persuade them to become involved. It is useful for young people to understand which of these strategies is their natural inclination. We then have a starting point from which they can try alternative strategies that will put them more in control of their body and their environment.

Before you begin

Read and photocopy the worksheets on pages 39–43, or have the young person write directly in this book.

Photocopy or draw the cards on page 117.

Have some water or a preferred drink and high-energy food like a banana or dried fruits available.

Collect: A timer, a CD or taped music for calming, a crossword book or puzzle book, comics, magazines or catalogues based on an interest of the young person.

Practice: For this section you do need to be confident about demonstrating 'breathe and blow'. Breathe onto the palm of your hand, move your hand away as you continue blowing. Demonstrate lengthening the breath as you count out to 4, then 6, then 8.

During the session

Work through pages 39–43.

To help the young person to alter their breathing, you need to teach activities that lead to an increase in arousal, e.g. running; walking fast; or any physical activity where you become breathless. Inside activities can be the stop-breathe-and-blow game equivalent to musical statues. Play the music, young people dance/jump around. When the music stops, hold up the visual card and model if need be: Stop, breathe and blow.

This then provides a good opportunity for drawing attention to, and talking about, heart rate, breathing and perspiration. You need to demonstrate how to then gain control of breathing. Show them how to do this by holding your own hand up and blowing on it, moving your hand away as the blowing continues. This gives a visual cue as to how long the blowing-out of the one breath is. You want to concentrate on making sure that it is long and slow. The young person can practise blowing on your hand and then on their own. Be aware that older students sometimes take a sharp intake of breath instead of blowing out, so emphasise the word *blow* rather than *breathe in*.

Other good ideas for practising blowing:

- Using a clock or watch with a second hand to encourage the young person to blow out and beat their last time.

- Blowing up a balloon or blowing out relighting birthday candles.

- Playing a game like blow football using straws and a ping-pong ball.

- Blowing bubbles.

Once the blowing is slow and steady, try facilitating blowing out in such activities with the visual prompt on page 117.

Look back at the pages on easy job/hard job. Talk about which jobs need a 'breathe and blow' reminder.

You might need to:

- Change the words we have used as these are based on our students descriptions of how they feel.

- Add some information that fight, flight and fear responses are a result of the body producing adrenaline.

- Explain that a flock response is when someone is drawn to others who might not being doing the right thing (acting out, challenging teachers).

Using the planner

Put any cut-up pictures into a plastic wallet, so they don't get lost.

When you make the plan for real-life situations, remember to agree what you will say to help. At times of high arousal the less said the better, and you may agree simply to show the card and model blowing out.

Breathe and blow to stay calm

Staying calm when things go wrong is important.

Stay calm and you can think...

What can I do here?
What are my choices?
What is my best choice?

The big question is:

How do I stay calm?

If you haven't already done this thinking, do it now:

When things go wrong I feel…

☐ Worried ☐ Scared ☐ Angry

What else?

☐ I feel hot.

☐ I feel squashed.

☐ I feel heavy.

☐ I feel buzzy.

☐ I feel panic.

☐ I can't think.

☐ 🖉 ....

When you feel any of these things your heart will beat faster. You heart beats fast and breathing is hard. When any of these things happen to you, it can help if *you have made a plan*.

I need to use my plan.

The very important thing you need to do is calm your breathing. Breathing in can be hard – try blowing out.

Blowing out then makes you breathe in.

You can read about this in the 'Getting worried, scared and angry' story on the next page.

You might still be worried, but now you can think and make a plan or use a plan that you have already made.

 'Breathe and blow' is a good strategy to learn.

☑ Blowing is good to help me stay calm.

☑ Blowing means I will also breathe in.

☑ Breathing in gets oxygen to my brain.

☑ My brain needs oxygen to help me think.

☑ Stay calm, keep thinking, stay in control.

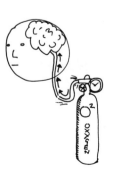

Getting worried, scared and angry

Sometimes I can get so worried. My head gets crazy. I get hot inside. I feel squashed. It's like I can't breathe. I want to hit and throw. Scared and angry. Like I am someone else.

I get angry and I can't think. Sometimes I want to think so I can make a plan. Make a plan to fix the problem. But I can't think. I can't think because I can't breathe. My heart beats faster and faster: it feels so big I think I might explode.

BUT! I breathe and I breathe in oxygen. Oxygen is in the air all around me. My brain uses the oxygen to help me think. My heart uses the oxygen and slows down.

Breathing in when I am mad can be really hard. My body is pretty smart. I can blow out and then this will help me to breathe in. I can think about blowing out and this will help me breathe in. Then I blow and I will breathe in and blow and breathe in and blow. Then I can think. I might still be worried, scared or angry, but now I can think and make a plan. Breathe and blow, that's my trick.

How to breathe and blow

It looks like this (kind of).

It sounds like a shh.

shh

You can change the sound to a sigh.

ahh

Practise blowing out to the count of 8.

1, 2, 3, 4, 5, 6, 7, 8

Learning to breathe and blow is important. You might need an adult to help you.

You can make a plan like this one:

When things get hard, I will try to breathe and blow.

When things get hard, other people can show me a card.

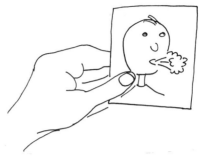

People can say... — Breathe and blow

They can breathe and blow with you.

Good choice

On page 117 is a 'breathe and blow' card. Copy this card and keep it in your planner. It may help you to remember to breathe and blow. The adults who help you may also want a copy of the card so that they can show it to you when you need help to try to breathe and blow.

Session 2.2: Plans to use gesture – notes for shapers

In this session

You will help the young person to become aware of how they can use touch in order to promote their own well-being, e.g. when we put our hand on our chest it helps us to regulate our breathing. Self-touch, or gesture, promotes well-being by using physical responses such as the release of oxytocin. Oxytocin is referred to as a well-being hormone.

Over time you may find that the 'breathe and blow' strategy is often paired with gesture. This is what happens in everyday practice: a calming breath is rarely taken without an accompanying gesture.

Before you begin

Read and photocopy the worksheet on page 46, or have the young person write directly in this book.

Photocopy or draw the cards on page 117.

For this section you do need to be confident about demonstrating hand on my head helps me think; hand on my chest helps me breathe and hand on my tummy helps me calm. Practise this and be clear about the examples you can give to explain when this is used, e.g. leaning on your hand when you are thinking.

During the session

Work through page 46.

Visual graphics are shown to the young person as they learn each gesture. In the session you can model using the gestures whenever you need to think, be calm or breathe. For example, put your hand on your head in an exaggerated thinking pose, accompanied by a thoughtful 'Hmm'; use hand on your chest when modelling 'breathe and blow' (previous session). You can model shoulders down, air exhalation and hands on your tummy when calm. Maybe with an 'I'm okay, I can do this'.

Using the planner

Put any cut-up pictures into a plastic wallet, so they don't get lost.

Encourage all adults who work with the young person to model and make the link for the young person:

> We are thinking. I want you
> to think. I can use a hand on
> my head to help me think.

To help consolidate this, adults can also be saying:

> You did great thinking. I really liked
> the way you put your hand on your
> head to help you think. When else
> will you need to think hard today?
> Let's write 'Hand on my head to
> help me think' on your timetable.

Plans to use gesture

Lots of people use their hands to help themselves keep calm and to help themselves think.

When we put our hands on our body, our body releases a 'feel-good' hormone that also helps us to feel calm.

☑ You can also hold your hands together to stay in control.

☑ Practise these gestures when you are calm.

☑ Practise these AND 'breathe and blow'.

If it seems like a good idea for you then use the cards on page 117.

Session 2.3: Plans to chill out – notes for shapers

In this session

'Plans to chill out' recognises that there are triggers in the environment that don't go away. Ultimately we want the young person to manage these triggers rather than losing control, but in the meantime it is a good strategy to make a plan that enables them to remove themselves for a short amount of time.

It's a strategy that mirrors what adults often do in their everyday life – to go outside for a breath of fresh air or a drink. The young people you work with may find it difficult to make connections between events and to replay their memories of these. So if they use a chill out plan, we need to make it explicit what they did and that this was successful, e.g. 'I liked the way you took a break'. Make it clear that the ultimate achievement in a chill out plan is returning to the original task at hand.

The chill out part of the plan is crucial because you must make the distinction between a plan to get out, chill out and other strategies that may look similar. Other such strategies could include *time out* (adult-introduced, removal from the situation because of inappropriate behaviour in a bid to reduce the behaviour) and *opting out* (the young person or student removes himself or herself from a situation but does not engage in any strategies to self-calm or to get back to the task at hand).

chill out has some features that mean a physiological response can occur:

- The young person goes to the *planned* place to calm on their own (you or another adult may monitor from a distance).

- You reinforce that the young person is being proactive in following their plan. You ensure that the plan has time restrictions on this and remind them to use their agreed calming strategy while there.

- Calming places are individualised, e.g. walking to calm in the exercise area or sitting to calm in a quiet area.

Some young people will choose activities they find calming that are also all-consuming. These won't work as a chill out plan. This is because the student needs to be able to disengage from the calming activity and return to the task at hand. Remember, as the shaper your task is to help them shape their thinking.

Before you begin

Read and photocopy the worksheets on pages 49–50, or have the young person write directly in this book.

Have some water or a preferred drink and high-energy food like a banana or dried fruits available.

Collect: A timer, music for calming, a crossword book or puzzle book, comics, magazines or catalogues based on an interest of the young person.

During the session

Work through pages 49–50.

Role-play is very important – not only at going to the agreed place to calm but practising the calming strategy in this place and then helping the young person to recognise when they are ready to return to the task. If you are using a timer, then make sure that the young person practises turning it to the agreed time and then using their plan to calm for the time agreed. It is only this practice that will tell you if the time is approximately right. Emphasise that it is this returning to the task which will make them ultimately successful.

Using the planner

Make sure that it is easy to find the chill out plan in the planner and practise using it. The student may want to make a special card that they can show when they are going to use their chill out plan.

Plans to get out, chill out

I am going to chill out.
Back soon.

You have already made some plans to calm:

☑ Breathe and blow

☑ Gesture

Sometimes things get hard. It can be hard to stay in the room and keep working. It can be hard to stay with the group and keep working. Sometimes we try to use our hands to keep calm and we are still worried, scared or angry. Sometimes we try to breathe and blow and we are still worried, scared or angry.

Here are other good ideas to try:

☑ Take time out in a quiet place.

☑ Go to your private place.

☑ Walk quickly to help you get a steady rate of breathing.

☑ Have a drink of water.

☑ Eat something like a banana.

☑ Listen to music.

☑ Read.

☑ Draw or write.

☑ ....

To try these you may need to have a get out, chill out plan.

You need to know what is calming so that you can use it to chill out in your chill out plan (see pp.118–119).

To make this plan you have to try this thinking:

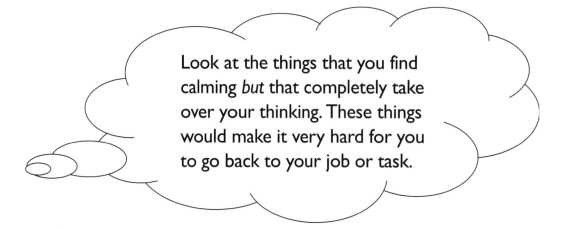

Look at the things that you find calming *but* that completely take over your thinking. These things would make it very hard for you to go back to your job or task.

It's important you know what these are. You can then:

☑ Choose not to put these in your get out, chill out plan because they might not help you to get back on task. Make another plan…

☑ Try to learn to do these activities for a set amount of time (say eight minutes – use a timer). This would mean that you could use them to calm down but then get back to work.

Plans to chill out mean that you:

• Plan where you will go.

• Plan what you will do to calm down and chill out.

• Plan to tell an adult where you are going. Remember that adults are there to keep you safe. The adult doesn't have to go with you but they do have to know where you are:

☑ Write the name of the person you will tell. ○○○ Who will I tell?

☑ Make a card that says:

I am going to…

I will be back in…

I am going to my room. Back in 20 minutes.

☑ Plan to get back to the task.

Session 2.4: Plans to wait – notes for shapers

In this session

Waiting seems to put young people under pressure because they don't know what to do when they wait. Knowing what to do includes being able to self-occupy in order to stay calm. 'Plans to wait' were developed specifically for this. It is essential to stay calm when you don't know how long you will wait.

The use of the waiting card can be made less obtrusive by making it smaller, by putting a calming picture on the back of it. How many of you hold your keys when you are waiting, or hold your handbag on your lap? These strategies can be adapted – with or without the waiting card. If it is a soft texture that the young person finds calming, then tie some fabric onto the keyring, or make a keyring from the fabric.

Before you begin

Read and photocopy the worksheets on pages 53–56, or have the young person write directly in this book.

Photocopy or draw the card on page 120.

During the session

Work through pages 53–56.

Set up some role-play scenarios with another adult that are likely to involve waiting. After an initial practice with you, ask the young person to take a message to this second adult. You will have primed this adult to ask the young person to wait while they first attend to something else.

Encourage the young person to think of waiting as something that needs their body to be still but their thinking to be busy: they can be busy thinking about their arms and legs (Are these still?); thinking about their breathing (Is it steady?); thinking about their thinking (Am I thinking 'I am waiting – I can do this?').

Prompt the young person's thinking by playing waiting games using the timer. 'We're waiting for three minutes – what will you choose?' Pair waiting with a positive reward.

Using the planner

Waiting is a difficult concept for a number of young people. In order to make an individualised plan you need to look at the work the young person has completed and identify and then clarify what helps them.

Keep the waiting card in the plastic wallet in the planner.

Plans to wait

Something to think about...

When you are waiting, you may feel worried, scared, or angry.

Staying calm can be really hard when you have to wait for someone or something. It can be easy to think:

These thoughts will make you worry! Worry leads to faster breathing. Faster breathing can make you panic.

So, going somewhere? Might have to wait?

You can make a plan to:

☐ Count backwards.

☐ Take something to look at.

☐ Listen to music.

☐ Draw or write.

☐ Talk to an adult.

Make a plan...

☑ Think…

I can do this. I can read, draw, listen to music.

☑ You can look at your watch and count backwards…

Six minutes… five minutes… four minutes…

If you are with an adult, the adult can count down for you:

I am waiting.
Sit still.
I can do this.
I can think of...

4
3
2
1

Waiting finished!

You could stick a picture of something that you like to think about on the back of your waiting plan.

Lots of adults get up and have a drink or something to eat to help them stay calm. You could always take something to eat and a bottle of water.

Think about this:

> Say you had an appointment with the doctor at 3:10pm. You arrived at 3:04pm. The receptionist said the doctor was *running to time*. This meant you were going to wait six minutes until 3:10pm. You had forgotten your book, or activity!

Now is a good time to breathe and blow.

Pretend the receptionist says:

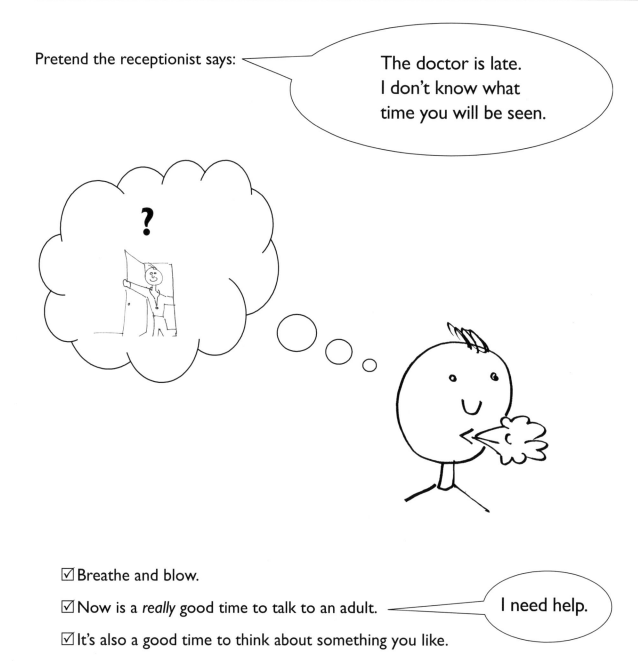

The doctor is late. I don't know what time you will be seen.

?

☑ Breathe and blow.

☑ Now is a *really* good time to talk to an adult.

I need help.

☑ It's also a good time to think about something you like.

You can make your own waiting card or use the one on page 120.

Topic 3: Plans to Be Organised

Session 3.1: Plans to organise my day
Session 3.2: Plans to organise my week
Session 3.3: Plans can change
Session 3.4: Plans to do a job

The **five key concepts** to communicate in these sessions:

1. Appointments are made for a set time, but sometimes start and finish late.

2. Plans can change.

3. Think 'breathe and blow' and practise asking for help.

4. Getting organised means writing down what to do and what to take.

5. Have a fun job to do after a hard job.

Session 3.1: Plans to organise my day – notes for shapers

In this session

'Plans to organise my day' is primarily about giving the young person some insight into daily planning. You can discuss who they will get to help them and agree when the plans will be made. There is a timetable sheet to help you plan and organise the day. As said before, some young people may want to adapt a regular filofax/diary.

Before you begin

Read and photocopy the worksheets on pages 60–64, or have the young person write directly in this book.

Photocopy page 121.

Find the list of hard jobs/easy jobs from Topic 1.

Copy a blank school timetable.

Photocopy or print from the internet examples of different types of timed day planners.

Talk to parents about after-school activities and appointments.

Start gathering information in order to clarify the rules about time in a number of settings, e.g. school, meal time at home, time allocated to free choice.

Find out about homework, household chores, directed leisure activities, so you can support thinking about okay jobs, hard jobs, easy, fun stuff.

Practise making plans to do jobs in different settings.

During the session

Work through pages 60–64.

Begin by supporting the person to list all of their tasks and activities. You then help them sequence the events/activities in the order that they happen. You are going to write in the process of getting ready with the activity that the young person is to do. An example of this is getting ready to catch a bus; you must allow a few minutes before you go to make sure you have money for the ticket, your keys and anything else you may need to take with you. Giving ourselves time to get ready and jotting down the things we need to take with us; these are all pieces of thinking that we need to show the young person how to do. At home we may plan to have our evening meal at 7pm but we know that the half hour before will be dedicated to preparation time. What we need to do is to timetable the strands of activities that relate to each other so that the person sees how other people organise it.

Be prepared to offer a good reward for completing hard/never-tried-before jobs. Help the young person identify a fun job that they will do later on in the day/week.

Using the planner

Begin the day with a planning-my-day session (call it whatever will be acceptable to the young person). This may only last 10–15 minutes. It is useful in teaching the person how to routinely check their day, and establish if anything has changed. This also provides an opportunity for them to record what they need to remember for different sessions e.g. *'This is hard I will need to breathe and blow'.*

The planner is a tool for the young person, but a number of other adults will become shapers and be responsible for maintaining its use. It might be time for you to review the resources that have been made and used. Meet with other relevant adults to have a discussion about the type of resource you are making with the young person, i.e. a planner, organiser, filofax and notebook.

Plans to organise my day

Organising your day means you can try to:

☑ plan in the evening for the next day

☑ ask an adult to help you:

☑ plan in the morning

Can you help me to make a plan for tomorrow?

Things to do today...

☑ ✏

Get up!
Pull-up duvet (makes Mum happy)
Wash face
Get dressed
Remember to brush hair
(makes me more attractive…)
Have breakfast
Clean teeth...
Get bag
Check money
Catch bus to school

Sometimes you have to be somewhere at a set time:

Classes at school start at set times.

Appointments (even though we can then be kept waiting!)

Your boss will say what time you have to start work.

What activities or appointments do you *have* to get to *on time*?

....

....

....

....

....

If getting places on time is hard for you, then write in when you need to leave for the appointment, class or activity.

What do you need to take with you?

Make a plan and write it down!

....

....

....

....

....

....

....

....

Getting organised means:

- thinking about what things you have to do

- writing these down in the order that they happen.

Remember to think:

What do I have to do?

then:

Which are the
easy, fun things.
I want to do...

Which are
hard jobs...

Which are okay...

Is *getting ready* an okay or a hard job? Maybe you have never planned to get ready for something. Planning when and how you will get ready for something can help you make the time to…

☑ look for your bus fare

☑ check you've brushed your teeth

☑ get anything you need to take with you

What time do I have to...?

Does this happen at a certain time?	What I have to do	Do I have to take anything?
12.45pm	Lunch at home	
By 1.25pm	Clean my teeth	
1.25pm	Get computer game	
1.30pm	Walk to computer club	Computer game

You can copy the timetable on page 121. Remember that organised people jot things like this down all the time. You might want to try to adapt a regular filofax.

To recap...

First, think of what you have to do and try to write these jobs down in the order that they happen. Remember the bit that is sometimes hard – you have to think about the things that you *want* to do'.

but you also have to think about the things that you *have* to do. Everyone has to keep themselves clean, everyone has to keep their room tidy and things like that. The plan to organise your day should help you make time to do all of these 'jobs'.

Then you will have time to do what you like to do.

Session 3.2: Plans to organise my week – notes for shapers

In this session

Plans for the week are really a platform to let students plan ahead. They can be great for preparing students for changes to their week. Such plans for change will be dealt with in Session 3.3. Weekly timetables in mainstream schools can be very overwhelming and visually confusing – even for teachers. Try colour-coding different sessions so that the pattern of the week can be seen more clearly.

Before you begin

Read and photocopy the worksheet on page 66, or have the young person write directly in this book.

Photocopy pages 122 and 123. Make sure coloured pens for colour-coding and adhesive tabs are available.

During the session

Work through page 66. You are helping the young person to see the process for planning *in action*:

What do I know should happen? Include activities like lunchtime and breaks.

Which of these are the same activity, repeated? Use the same colour to mark these.

Try to anticipate which timetabling issues could prove difficult. A student who hates Maths will need to have any positives pointed out to them – 'Look, it's followed by a break (easy job?) or a favourite subject, it's only a single session'.

Using the planner

Plans to organise my week need to be scheduled into the young person's weekly routine – some prefer it first thing at the beginning of a week. It can be seen as the precursor to planning the first day of the week. So, on the first day of the week, I will start by looking at the plan for my week and then I can plan today.

The reality for organised people is that they need to think about the week ahead before Monday morning – some on a Sunday evening. Whenever the time, it will be most successful if it is timetabled in. Also have an action plan should this not happen because, for example, the young person is late to school.

Plans to organise my week

On page 122 is a sheet to help you plan and organise your week. You can use your weekly plan to help you plan for the week ahead. During school terms and during most of the year if you work, the weeks can look a lot the same.

At school, your lessons for the term will occur at the same time each day. If you have after-school activities, these are likely to happen on the same days. If your parents work regular days, then this is not likely to change from week to week.

Planning with an adult can be helpful. Include all of your school tasks/activities/sessions and then other appointments. You can then see spaces for the things you like to do. You may want help to colour-code the different sessions you have at school; or maybe the days that you need to take your sports kit.

The types of things that change, week by week are more likely to be:

☑ having people (family friends or relatives) visit your house

☑ visiting people at their homes

☑ going out to eat, movies…

☑ when assignments are due

☑ going on school camp/excursions/holidays

☑ parents working shifts or irregular hours

Laminating your weekly timetable can also be helpful. Then when you have activities that change each week, like going to the movies, or having friends visit, you can mark these with an adhesive note, or a dry-wipe marker.

You can also use the important information form on page 123 to jot down exactly that – stuff you need to remember…

☑ Mr Thompson will be away next Wednesday…

☑ Bring in newspaper for art

Importantly, having a weekly timetable lets you see when there's a change.

Session 3.3: Plans can change – notes for shapers

In this session

'Plans can change' is really about providing the young person with appropriate levels of support to understand and accept change. Accepting change to an established routine, or to a favoured activity or the unexpected absence of a preferred adult can be difficult. In the initial plan you can agree on a particular colour that will help to signify there is a change. The colour or word prompts the connection to use a calming strategy in preparation for a change. Some people may also require a lead-in period of time to accept the change. Presenting change visually will not alter this, so always try to give as much notice as you can. Your mantra could be:

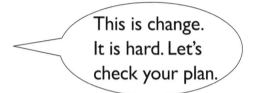

This is change. It is hard. Let's check your plan.

When preparing for change, it may be that you need to think about other parts of the day or week – is there some room for flexibility so that the person can engage in a particularly enjoyable activity to compensate for a particularly disappointing change? The use of the easy jobs list can be useful – especially if you have split it into easy and fun jobs. Remember to try to judge the scale of disappointment from the person's perspective – an outing being postponed may actually be a cause for celebration for the young person on the spectrum!

Before you begin

Read and photocopy the worksheets on pages 69–70, or have the young person write directly in this book.

Have card ready to make 'a change card'.

Have list of fun jobs (page 31) ready and to hand.

Think about novel alternatives that you could suggest when the young person is making a plan for change.

During the session

Work through pages 69–70.

Remaining positive, while also acknowledging how difficult change can be, can be a difficult balance. Try to remember that planning for the change won't mean that the young person will *like* the change, but just that there is another course of action which may help to distract them.

Using the planner

Sharing the plans for change with colleagues, including any mantras they may need to use, is key to increasing success by minimising the young person's anxiety.

Plans can change

Using a weekly plan can help you see when something you planned to do has to change. Sometimes things change – even after you have written them down!

Changes can be hard. If you can see the change, sometimes it can help. Seeing the change can help you get used to the change – even though you may not like it!

Adults can highlight the changes by writing them in a different colour:

☑ Now could be a good time to think about your plan to calm…

☑ It can also help you plan to do something else…

Adults can be good at helping you to think of something else to do when plans have to change. Planning with an adult can be a good thing to try.

✎ Which adult will you ask?

....

Plan for change:

☑ How will you keep calm?

I am going to chill out. Back soon.

☑ Now look at this list of fun jobs you could do instead:

....

....

....

....

....

....

....

Session 3.4: Plans to do a job – notes for shapers

In this session

It can help young people enormously to see a task or job that they must do broken down into steps. As with all aspects of the planner, what we want is for the young person to try this, see if it helps them and then to be able to ask others to help them by writing down the steps to a task.

Before you begin

Think about a job that is relevant for the young person that can be done in a short space of time. Write out the task instructions. This means all the small steps:

- What the job is

- Equipment needed

- What you need to say to ask for help

- How you know the job is finished.

Find a suitable motivational reward available for completion of the job.

Read and photocopy the worksheets on pages 73–74, or have the young person write directly in this book.

Photocopy pages 124 and 125.

Create eight cards by drawing or copying page 126.

In this session

Work through pages 73–74.

Have the young person try out the job you have planned, using the task instruction.

Your role is:

- to help the person learn the value of having a task broken down into easy-to-achieve steps

- to help the young person value their ability to complete tasks independently when the steps of the task are drawn or written down.

Once you have addressed these, you can support the young person to look at their instructions and go through a process of self-monitoring: 'Do I know what I am supposed to do?' You can do this by:

- teaching to the task sheets in the planner

- including one deliberately unintelligible instruction in a task of several steps. This then provides the opportunity for you to shape the young person's responses.

When students don't understand what they are to do, we want to teach them to keep calm and to ask for help.

Using the planner

We all assume that young people will be able to remember what to do. Usually they can, but by forgetting one small step in the task, things can go very wrong. In the workplace checklists are commonly used where a job has to be done to a standard.

It's useful to contact a local hotel, retailer or garage for an example of forms they use for checking a job is done and use this adult format in the planner.

A system can be set up to enable the young person to use plans to do a number of different jobs. This system can dovetail the daily timetable with the step-by-step instructions. Ultimately we may aim for all instructions to be held together in the planner. However, this isn't always possible – either because it is too bulky or because the young person cannot manage it. The instructions may instead be put in a file which the young person has easy access to.

Plans to do a job

Got a job to do?

You have already started thinking about easy, okay and hard jobs. In your day or your week you may have many different jobs to do. The following tips can help you plan how to do your jobs:

☑ Get an adult to write down the steps of the job

☑ Check what the adult wrote first then

☑ Do the job.

Try the job that the adult suggests – use the written instructions.

Use pages 124 and 125 to help you plan your jobs. Check first:

- Read what the adult has written. The adult can write your job on a page like pages 124 and 125 (or on any piece of paper).

- 'Check out' what they have written:

You can think and check:

> Can I do this?

If not then ask:

> Can you help me?

> Do I know who can help me?

If not then ask:

> Who can I ask if I need help?

> Do I know when I am finished?

If not then ask:

> When will I be finished?

When you have a job to do, here's a thinking tip:

> Ahhh, I can do this. I've done it before

- Okay job or a job I've done a lot

> Keep calm. Read my instructions I know I can ask for help

- A job I don't like

> Keep calm and *think*. I can ask for help.

> I've never done this before. Can you write it down? Can you show me? Can you help me?

- A job I've never done before

Use the cards on page 126 to show the adult.

Topic 4: Plans to Be with People

Session 4.1: Plans for too much noise

Session 4.2: Plans to ask for help

Session 4.3: Plans to use public words in public places

Session 4.4: People plans

The **five key concepts** to communicate in these sessions:

1. Tell an adult when they talk too much. Ask the adult to 'write it down'.

2. Tell an adult when you are worried, scared or angry.

3. You don't have to remember everything – use the planner as a reminder.

4. Organised people practise saying things that are difficult – they write down the words they need to use as a reminder.

5. Practise 'think it, don't say it' when you want to use a personal or private word in a public place.

Session 4.1: Plans for too much noise – notes for shapers

In this session

'Plans to be with people' was devised to address the well-documented difficulties young people on the spectrum have in interacting with others in a crowded or busy area. The first issue covered is the need to give the young person the strategies to manage the noise that other people make. Many young people become anxious in response to the communication styles of others, just as they may become anxious in the presence of too much background noise. While it may not always be possible to alter this, you can teach the young person appropriate coping strategies.

Before you begin

Read and photocopy the worksheets on pages 78–81, or have the young person write directly in this book.

Photocopy page 126 to make into cards; if you want some ideas for making the students own cards, look at page 80.

Review the different spaces that young people work in and identify the sort of adjustments that it might be possible to suggest. Often in large rooms, talk is perceived as noise.

Look in the planner and gather the resources that have been successful or might be worth reviewing again.

Have 'breathe and blow' cards, 'I need a break' cards, and 'think it, don't say it' cards to hand.

During the session

Work through pages 78–81.

Begin by working with the young person to identify which physical reactions they experience (e.g. heart beating faster, increase in breathing, perspiration, maybe a sensation of their head about to explode) in response to the talking of others.

You need to help the young person:

- to recognise that this response is understandable

- to know that they do have choices about the way that they then respond

- it should be seen as an empowering strategy. Again, role-play is key.

When looking at practising the plans in real life, see if you can work with the young person to identify which adults are *easy to talk with* or *hard to talk with*.

Encourage the young person to practise their skills with people they find easy to talk with and build up to using the plans with those who are more difficult to talk with.

See if the young person can predict which comment they may want to say to which people. This can help them to plan and to role-play.

Using the planner

Put any cut-up pictures into a plastic wallet, so they don't get lost.

When you make the plan for real-life situations, remember to agree what you will say or do to help the young person. Prompt them to look in their planner:

> They talk fast. Let's see if there's something we can find in your planner.

Plans for too much noise

It can be tough being with other people.

Other people can be unpredictable and confusing.

Everyday, *some* time has to be spent with other people.

It can be hard to work out what they think and what they mean.

> I find it hard to be with other people when...

✎ ...all they do is talk

....

....

....

....

....

....

Dealing with all their noise!

Some people talk a lot. It can be tiring to listen to a lot of talking.

Some people talk too fast. It can be really hard to keep up with all they say. Sometimes their words become jumbled.

Sometimes people can make a lot of noise!

Sometimes when people talk to me I just don't understand what they say. Sometimes it is because I can't keep up with their fast talking. Sometimes I don't understand the words that they use or the way that they say things.

A talking tip

When it feels like this:

What do you think when people talk too much or you don't understand?

You can try to:

☑ Ask the person to write what they are saying.

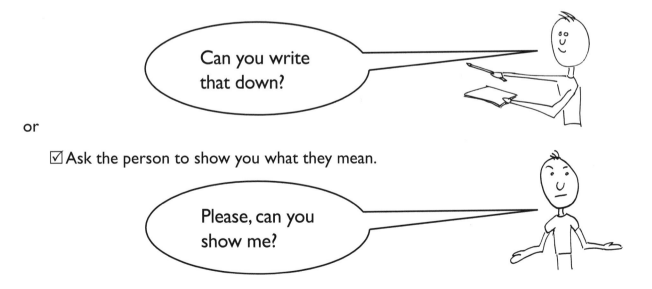

Can you write that down?

or

☑ Ask the person to show you what they mean.

Please, can you show me?

or

☑ Say that you need to leave the room/activity/area.

or

☑ Ask the person to repeat what they said – slowly.

or

☑ Maybe something like…

Sometimes, when people:

☑ talk too much

☑ talk too fast

☑ are too noisy or

☑ use words that you don't understand

you can feel worried, scared or angry.

If this happens to you then your breathing can become fast and shallow.

You have to let the person know. This can be really difficult. *Showing* the person can come in useful. Showing someone is a good way to communicate at times like this. You can cut out the cards on page 126 and keep them in the pocket of your planner, wallet, or in your pocket.

Try it and see if it suits you.

You might even want to write your own cards.

Session 4.2: Plans to ask for help – notes for shapers

In this session

Having plans to ask for help encourages young people to take charge of their learning. The young person needs to work independently but be able to ask for help when necessary.

Before you begin

Read and photocopy the worksheet on page 84, or have the young person write directly in this book.

Photocopy page 127.

Investigate the particular situations where the young person does not ask for help when they need to.

During the session

Work through page 84.

Once the young person has the idea, the plans can be adapted to ask for help in particular circumstances, e.g. when shopping. The interaction pattern looks something like this:

1. Look for the appropriate person e.g. shop assistant.

2. Say 'Excuse me'.

3. Wait for the person to say: Yes?

4. I will try to say: I need help to...

Obviously, you may need to build in a plan for when someone doesn't answer (say it again/ask another assistant). In this example, the acknowledgement the shop assistant has given to 'Excuse me', is written as 'Yes?' In reality this will vary depending on culture and situation. Your judgement will be needed to decide what people are most likely to respond with. It may be 'How can I help you?' or it may be 'What?'

Using the planner

Decide which sheets from this session will be a useful part of the planner.

Put the cards into a plastic wallet in the planner or laminate them and attach to a keyring.

Plans to ask for help

One of the good things about other people is that they can help you when things get hard. Sometimes people won't know that you need help. So first you have to ask for help. Look at each step and have a think:

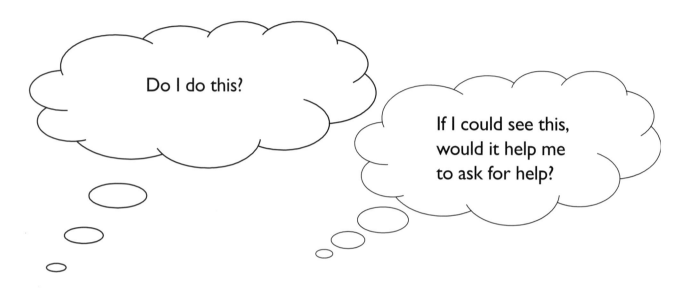

You can ask an adult to video you in a lesson that you find hard. Watch yourself on the video when you need help. This will help you see what you really do when you need help.

If you think it might help, then copy page 127 and keep it in your planner.

Session 4.3: Plans to use public words in public places – notes for shapers

In this session

Plans to use public words is about learning which words are personal and private and which words are okay to use in general public and with most people. Sometimes young people do not understand that certain phrases are acceptable at home, maybe within their family, but are not acceptable in the workplace or at school.

It is important to recognise that inappropriate language can be a response to stress. In these situations, the most effective action is to reduce the stressor. This will then reduce the anxiety and so the inappropriate language.

Sometimes the use of private or personal words can elicit a response of indignation. To try to ensure that such language is not then used again to elicit this response, it is best to try to under-respond to such language. This can be very difficult, especially for new staff or people who are unfamiliar with the young person. Sometimes the young person may ask particularly personal questions. In this circumstance it can be helpful for all people to have the same mantra of:

That's personal.
It's finished.

This is said with no emotion. The adult then turns and directs their attention to something other than the young person.

Before you begin

Read and photocopy the worksheets on pages 87–88, or have the young person write directly in this book.

Photocopy the 'think it, don't say it' graphic on page 138.

Investigate the particular situations where the young person does not ask for help when they need to.

Gather information on the types of words that the student uses, with whom and in which circumstances.

During the session

Work through pages 87–88.

Be aware that sometimes when an adult says the words which we refer to as private, a young person can become excitable. Writing the words down and referring to them as 'this word' or 'this', whilst pointing to the word, can be one way to help avoid this.

Using the planner

All adults can refer the young person to their list when they use a private word in public. If the list already has an alternative, then the young person can be reminded that this is a suitable alternative. It may be that rewards need to be attached to the use of public words.

Plans to use public words in public places

When talking gets hard you can use the wrong types of words.

There are words that can be used anywhere and with anyone – old people, small children and people you don't know. These words are 'everyday' words and they will not upset other people.

We call these *public* words.

Private words can be more difficult to get right. They can upset other people. They can be words such as swear words, but are not only obscene or swear words. There are also words that can upset people because they are *personal*. This means that they are about the way that people look or smell or are about the things that they do, or the things that they believe in.

An adult can help you to make a list of words and help you think if these words are private, public or personal. If these are words you need to try *not* to say then fill in the list on page 128 and keep it in your planner. Now is a good time to:

Think it, don't say it.

There's a 'think it, don't say it' card on page 138. You can copy it for your planner. Adults who are helping you may want one for their own kit.

Private or personal??????

Sometimes I get angry and sometimes I get worried and sometimes I just want to let someone else know what I think.

Sometimes I might want someone else to feel bad, or shocked.

There are public words I can use to do this. And there are words that are private or personal. I try not to use private or personal words. I try not to use private or personal words when I am with…

....

An adult can help me by showing this to me:

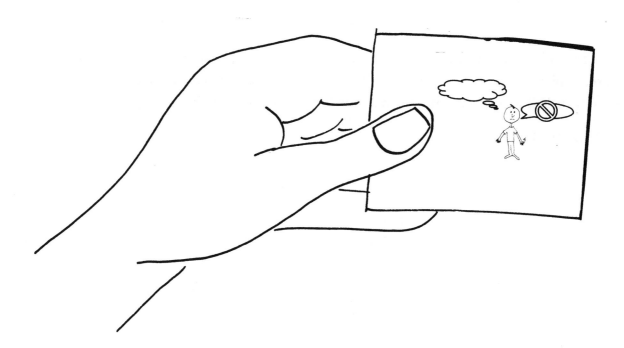

or to remind me to:

make a good choice

Session 4.4: People plans – notes for shapers

In this session

> Addressing the social communication skills of a person with an autistic spectrum disorder is a huge challenge. This session looks at how the young person could work to do this. There may need to be additional sessions where the young person goes through this process with the chosen adult.

> In this session there are three steps. The first looks at working out what the young person wants to learn to do differently. The communication and interaction is then broken down into a short script that can be practised in a safe environment. The final step is to practise what has been learnt in real conversations and interactions.

Before you begin

> Read and photocopy the worksheets on pages 92–94, or have the young person write directly in this book.

> Photocopy pages 129–135.

> Think about which plans might be most useful for the young person.

> You might find it helpful to discuss particular communication issues with colleagues such as experienced educators, speech-language pathologists and psychologists who can support you.

During the session

> Work through pages 92–94.

> Use the steps on pages 93–94 to focus on one communication issue and break it down step-by-step. Here is an example of how to say hello:

> Walk to… (person's name e.g. Max)

> Stand still

> Say:
> Stand still
> Wait (breathe and blow)

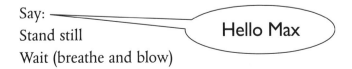

Hello Max

Listen for Max to say:
Tell Max my news.

Hello

Then model what the sequence looks like. As with other aspects of Learning to Plan, have the person role-play, video and then complete real-world practice.

When you role-play and video you can incorporate 'good practice' and 'dodgy practice'. Use whatever words you wish – sometimes young people respond to 'thumbs-up' and 'thumbs-down'. The notion is the same – you too can do it wrong and then you can receive the feedback from the young person.

If you have time, try the examples of plans to be with people from pages 129–135. One is a plan for interrupting, the second is a plan for being told what to do.

Using the planner

Once the young person is comfortable role-playing the scenario, you need to encourage them to put it into actual practice and to refer back to their planner if they need help. It is one thing to know to wait for the person to answer before you say anything. It is a completely different thing to practise doing this!

Practice is the key for you to modify the step-by-step instructions you have made together. There may be particular aspects that the person finds extremely difficult. These may need to be practised out-of-sequence. As with all aspects of the planner, the greatest outcome of the young person knowing what they are learning is gener-alisation of that skill. If the young person is practising how *to wait* for someone to greet them, then you can make the connection with another task such as learning *to wait* for someone to answer a question. Not necessarily any easier, but you will have made the connection for the young person.

Remember when we waited for Max to say hello? Today we will practise standing still and waiting for Sam to tell us the answer.

The list of possible 'plans to be with people' is endless. The following are simply suggestions:

- a plan to agree the game

- a plan to take turns

- a plan to ask someone to play with me

- a plan for when I lose a game

- a plan for when I win a game

- a plan to share food at a party table

- a plan to say if I don't know how to play the game

- a plan to ask for help when something is lost

- a plan to ask for help when I don't know what to do

- a plan to answer the telephone (at home)

- a plan to answer the telephone (at work)

- a plan to say I have an ASD

- a plan to ask for a reminder

- a plan to knock and enter a room with a closed door

- a plan to ask someone to pass the salt or pepper.

People plans

Making people plans is about having a plan that helps you – in some way – to be with other people.

You need to find a person who is either:

☑ your Mum or Dad

☑ an adult at school

☑ family friend

You can try to say:

> Can you help me make a plan? A plan to help me at home.

> Can you help me make a plan? A plan to help me at work.

> Can you help me make a plan? A plan to help me at school.

The adult will want to find out:

☑ what is hard

☑ who it is hard to do this with

Sometimes this person might see that you find something hard.

It can be hard to:

☑ meet people

☑ say hello

☑ interrupt people

☑ answer when someone says something to you

If this person sees that something is hard for you they might say to you:

It can be difficult to interrupt... Let's make a plan to help you interrupt.

or

I will tell my friends what your name is. It would make me feel happy if you said hello to my friends when I told them your name. Let's try to make a plan to help you say hello.

It can be hard when someone tells you what to do. At work your boss will say what to do. Let's make a plan of what you can say when s/he does.

So how do you make plans to live, play and work with people?

Step 1.
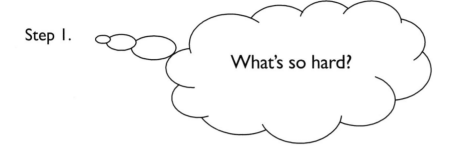

What's so hard?

First you need to find out what it is, that is so hard.

Step 2.
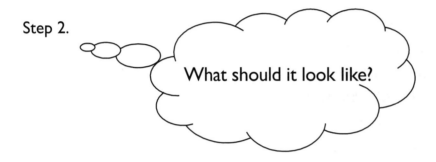

What should it look like?

What exactly should you be trying to do and say instead?

Step 3. Can the task be broken down into steps? You learn by reading (and doing) the written instructions, step-by-step. You learn what to do and what to say step-by-step.

Step 4. Remember to include your calming strategies.

Step 5. Then practise, practise, practise.

Give yourself a reward…

Topic 5: Plans to Think

Session 5.1: Plans to think when things go well and when things go wrong
Session 5.2: Plans for when you are worried, scared or angry
Session 5.3: Plans to sort it out
Session 5.4: Plans to succeed

The **five key concepts** to communicate in these sessions:

1. Breathe and blow – oxygen helps you think clearly.

2. Use your chill out card when you need a thinking break.

3. When things go wrong, ask an adult to write down what happened.

4. When adults give you praise ask them to write down what you did right.

5. Remember you can Stop and think/stop and choose.

Any of these key concepts which a young person finds useful, can be mantras to share with other supporting adults:

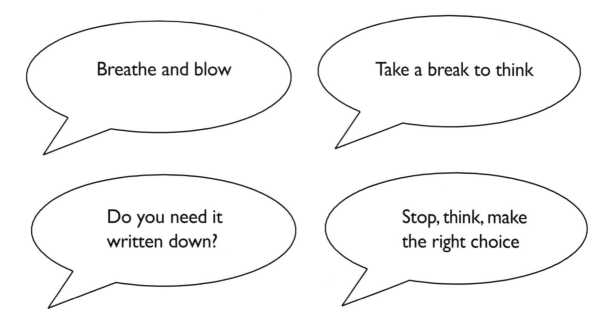

Breathe and blow

Take a break to think

Do you need it written down?

Stop, think, make the right choice

Session 5.1: Plans to think when things go well and when things go wrong – notes for shapers

In this session

Making plans is a great way to work out what skills to practise. Sometimes it is what young people think (or don't think!) that means their plans don't work. We know that young people struggle to think about things that have happened. This may be because they can't remember. It may be because they haven't exactly understood the chain of events. Making plans to think about what has happened – great things they have done as well as those things that are more disappointing – may prove key to the success of them learning from their experiences.

Before you begin

Read and photocopy the worksheets on pages 98–101, or have the young person write directly in this book.

Photocopy pages 136 and 137.

During the session

Work through pages 98–101.

The introduction on page 98 reinforces the notion of the young person being facilitated to take charge of their actions and their learning. It also highlights the importance of the young person learning to find out what they did that was so positive. This increases the chance of this

- being incorporated into another plan and

- happening again.

Using the planner

It can be easy to complete this session with the young person and then move on. However, there are straightforward ways to incorporate it into your practice:

- After praise or a reward, ask the young person 'What did you do that was so great?'

- Get the young person to write down what they have achieved. This will help reinforce it and ensure they have personalised it – 'I am good at...', 'I did a good job of...'. It's up to you to make sure that it's done in a way that is meaningful and not patronising.

Plans to think when things go well and when things go wrong

You have learnt how to make some really good plans.

Being in charge of your own actions means making plans to:

☑ be calm

☑ get organised and know what is going on

☑ be with other people.

☑ Planning to be in control means writing things down.

☑ Staying in control means staying calm.

☑ Stay calm and you can start to think about solving (sorting out) problems.

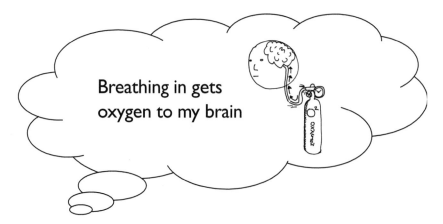

Breathing in gets oxygen to my brain

When things go right and you feel excited, or when things go wrong and you get worried, scared or angry:

it can be hard to remember what has happened

it can be hard to work out what you did that worked

and what you did that maybe wasn't so great.

It can be easier to think about these things if you can see them written down.

So, you might need to make a plan to help you think:

☑ after something great has happened

Huh? after something *great* has happened?

Yes, because if you don't know what it was that you did that was so good, you may not know what to do again, next time!

and

☑ when something is going wrong.

When something good has happened, people often say

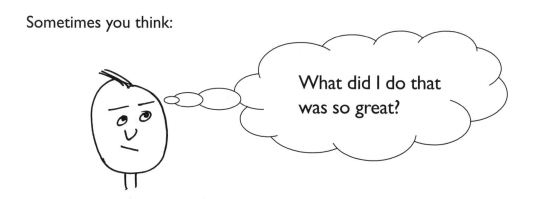

Well done!   or   That was brilliant!!   or   I wish you did that more often!!

Sometimes you think:

What did I do that was so great?

If people tell you why you did the right thing you can:

    ☑ do it again

    ☑ do it with other people or in new situations.

Of course you can ask...

> Did I do a good job?
> Tell me what I did?

Copy pages 136 and 137 and you can keep a list of what you are learning and what you do that is good.

Session 5.2: Plans for when you are worried, scared or angry – notes for shapers

In this session

This section is about planning for future blips or times of crisis. This planning is often helped by reflecting on past experiences.

Before you begin

Read and photocopy the worksheets on pages 104–107, or have the young person write directly in this book.

Photocopy or draw the cards on page 138.

Be clear about the what the young person does when scared, worried or angry. These may not be extreme behaviours. They might be low-grade but disruptive behaviours, such as giggling or noise making.

During the session

Work through pages 104–107.

This is a good opportunity to demonstrate your willingness to consider the young person's perspectives. It is also a good opportunity to make explicit which behaviours are acceptable and which are unacceptable:

Yes it is awful to feel scared, worried, angry.

I know it can stop you making good choices.

Hitting, kicking, throwing, ignoring instructions, running away are not good choices.

It is not okay to hit, kick, throw…

If you hit, kick, throw…at school, then you will…

If you hit, kick, throw…at work, then you will… (e.g. lose your job).

If you hit, kick, throw…in public then you will… (e.g. be arrested).

The session also allows for discussion about how you will try to help the young person at such times. Include what you will do, what you will say. This session may be only part of the process. Explain that you will both try out the plan and that it may need further fine-tuning.

The examples given on page 107 are only examples and will need to be personalised for the young person you are working with.

Using the planner

Keep the plans in the planner and photocopy any graphics that you may need in your kit. Remember that the plans are work-in-progress. As the young person becomes more proficient at keeping calm, they can become more able to make good choices at times of crisis.

Plans for when you are worried, scared or angry

When something is going wrong…talking doesn't always help.

Remember you can:

☑ use your chill out plan

☑ use you cards to ask adults for help

☑ write it down on a piece of paper

Getting organised means working with an adult to help you make a plan to help you when things are actually *going* wrong.

An adult can show you a picture or show some words that will help you to make the right choice at that time.

When you need to learn something you can rehearse what to do. This is called role-play. You are pretending.

Say, you were really angry and wanted to throw a chair. This is a really serious *example*.

If you throw the chair, things will get worse – you might break something or you might hurt someone. This would be very serious and you will be in **trouble**.

At the time, you feel worried, scared or angry.
It can be hard to do that thinking!

This is where an adult can show you one of the cards that will help you think.

This card is on page 138, copy it if you need to. It would help to have your plan to calm on the back – like the 'breathe-and-blow' picture.

Sometimes when you are scared, worried or angry you need someone else to remind you what your choices are. An adult can write in the box what a good choice would be and what the other (not so good) choice/s would be.

If you were holding the chair up high, a good choice would be to put the chair down.

The not-so-good choice would be to keep holding it up. But you might not feel safe enough to put the chair down.

So, another good choice would be to ask the person to go away. Then you could put the chair down.

The adult is worried… ○ ⬭ ⬬ He's going to break something or hurt someone.

The adult shows the card:  STOP ! Think 👍 Make a good choice

The adult might say: I am going away.

You can say:  Go away. Then I'll put the chair down.

The adult might think of this as a good choice for you and write it on this card:

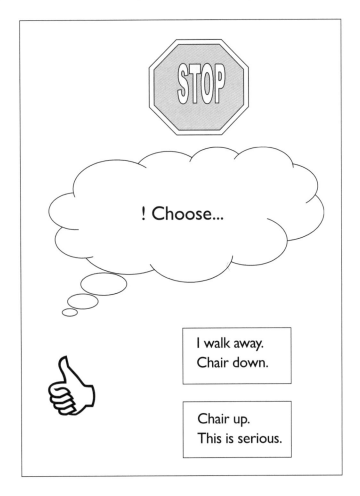

Holding a chair up is an example of very serious behaviour. Other examples of what you might do when you are worried, scared or angry could be:

✎ refusing to do the job ....

running away ....

....

....

....

....

....

....

Session 5.3: Plans to sort it out – notes for shapers

In this session

A process for sorting out when things have gone really wrong is introduced. This process can also be thought of as a debrief. The session also refers to 'making it right', which allows for discussion about sanctions and consequences.

The procedure you use must be based on your organisation's policy. You will need to ensure that the suggestions we make are acceptable to the organisation.

Before you begin

Read and photocopy the worksheets on pages 110–111, or have the young person write directly in this book.

Photocopy pages 139–140.

Be clear of your organisation's policies. Discuss with a senior member of staff, what the options for the debriefs are.

During the session

Work through pages 110–111.

You can also discuss the example of a plan to sort it out on page 139 and try using page 140 to make your own plan.

Using the planner

You might want to make several copies of page 140 and have them in the planner in case they are needed.

'Plans to sort it out' is a process to help the young person think about events, and ultimately learn from an experience or incident. These often refer to experiences or incidents that are challenging situations.

In order for the plans to be successful the debrief with the student needs to become routine. They are mediated by an adult who remains in a neutral, facilitative role. Therefore, if an adult is involved in the incident, it may be more appropriate for another adult to facilitate the debrief. The adult who witnesses or is involved in an incident can give the young person a written direction such as: 'This is serious', 'We have to sort it out', 'Meet in the debrief area (specify e.g. meeting room) in 10 minutes – 12.10pm'.

Mantras at this time may be:

You can build in time before a debrief occurs by having the young person complete a written or drawn account of what they recall happened. In many organisations, adults will be required to complete a written record of any incidents. In order for the debrief to be viewed as useful and positive by the young person, you need to ensure that the young person is always heard. This is not the same as always agreeing with them. Tools that can make this helpful is to say things like:

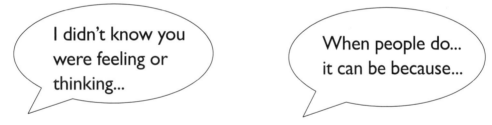

Making the issues less personal can also help:

What is important is that difficulties or triggers that arise from a difference in the way the young person thinks are identified.

'Plans to sort it out' makes the process explicit. Consistency and transparency can decrease the fear associated with this. This does not mean there are no consequences or sanctions for the young person, should that be appropriate. However, the emphasis is in making a plan to help the person change the outcome, should the situation arise again.

Plans to sort it out

Sometimes, things go wrong.

When things go wrong you may feel a whole lot of things. You might also be worried, scared or angry. Thinking when you are worried, scared or angry can be hard.

It is a good idea to try to think about what happened when you are calm – this might be at school or at home. Sometimes adults will give you a special time or place to do this thinking.

You might think you *know* why things went wrong. Sometimes what *you* think happened and what somebody else thinks happened, are very different. Making a time to think about it with an adult means that the adult can do a bit of detective work before you meet.

What went wrong?

When you meet, the adult can help you to:

- 🖉 draw what happened
- 🖉 write what happened
- 🖉 see the problem

You can make a plan to sort it out. Sorting it out can mean making a plan to try to do it differently next time.

You need to think and write down:

✏ Which adults can help you to sort it out?

....

....

....

✏ Where will you meet to sort it out? Is there only one place possible? Are there several places you can go to sort it out?

....

....

....

Sorting it out means doing good thinking about:

☑ what you were thinking

☑ what you were feeling

☑ what other people were thinking

☑ what other people were feeling

Then you can 'put it right'. 'Putting it right' means that you might have to:

☑ say sorry

☑ explain what you were thinking

☑ pay for some damage

☑ do a job that tells other people you are sorry

Other ways of 'putting it right' might be...

✏

....

....

....

You can also make a plan in case things go wrong again. On pages 139 and 140 are examples of plans. You can make your own plans.

Session 5.4: Plans to succeed – notes for shapers

In this session

Plans to succeed are about building self-belief in the young person. A belief that they can do what they plan to do. As the shaper, you are working to help them see what they have achieved. Help them to build memories of positive experiences.

Before the session

Read and photocopy the worksheets on pages 113–114, or have the young person write directly in this book.

Photocopy page 141.

Gather evidence of the plans achieved so far – this may be photos but could also include positive reinforcement charts if these have been used.

During the session

Work through pages 113–114.

You can list plans that the young person has used in real life even with support from an adult. Then you can add 'independently' or 'by myself' later, when they can do it without any help.

Feel free to be as creative as you can – use photographs, wall displays, anything to remind the young person of all that they can do. Especially when they have planned and practised for their achievements.

Using the planner

Incorporate looking at this 'I can do' list when winding down for the week and when planning for the week ahead. Advise other adults of the list so that they can use this to talk about the positives with the young person. Many of our young people do not always offer up information on their latest achievements. 'Plans to succeed' can be used by all adults to ensure that they can embrace and celebrate the young person's success with them.

Plans to succeed

You know how to make plans. Plans that will help you:

- ☑ stay calm when you are worried, scared or angry. Staying calm helps because then you can think about what to do.

- ☑ be organised. Being organised can help you stay calm.

- ☑ ask for help – other people can help you out! Find an adult to help you make your plans.

- ☑ make good choices.

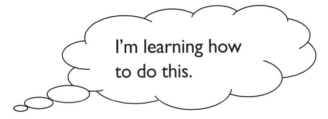

You have some plans. You have to try to make them happen. This means role-play and real-life practice.

Keep practising and you will learn to carry out your plan. Remember:

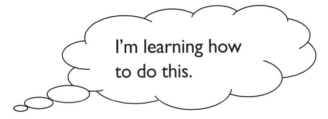

I'm learning how to do this.

When you use your plans, you need to:

and think:

Hey, I can do this....
I am amazing!

And you know, when things get hard it can be easy to forget how amazing you are.

To succeed in using your plans:

1. Work with an adult (use page 141).

2. Write or draw in all the things that you can do *now*. Some will be easy. Some will be hard.

3. Look at this list when things are hard.

    ☑ make a plan

    ☑ practise my plan

    ☑ use my plan

    ☑ write it down!

    ☑ know I can do it

Good for you!

Photocopiable Sheets
for a Personal Planner

My okay jobs

Easy Jobs	Fun Jobs

Cards to stay calm

Hand on my stomach
helps me relax

Hand on my head
helps me think

Hand on my chest
helps me breathe

Breathe and blow

A plan to get out, chill out

1

2 I will try to: (✎ your choice)

3

A plan to get out, chill out (continued)

Where will I go?
Who will I tell?

4   I plan to tell ....

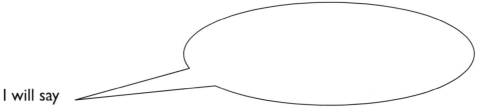

5   I will say

6   I can write it down

Going for a walk to
the shop, be back in
about half an hour.

7   I will try to use my plan to calm.

Return to the task.

I have made my own plan.
Good choice

A plan to wait

My plans for the day

Day or date...

Does this happen at a certain time?	What I have to do	Do I have to take anything?	Who could help me?

My plans for the week

When?	Monday	Tuesday	Wednesday	Thursday	Friday	Saturday	Sunday

Important information

Stuff to remember

A plan to do a job

Job:...

☑ Equipment I will need to do the job:

....

....

....

☑ Where to do the job:

....

....

....

☑ Who I can ask to help:

....

....

....

☑ The job will be finished when:

....

....

....

☑ My reward will be:

....

....

Steps of the job

If you write the steps in my job, then I can try to do it by myself

....

....

....

....

....

....

....

....

....

....

....

....

....

....

....

....

....

....

Communication cards

Can you write that down?

I need to go outside.

Please, can you show me?

Can you tell me that again?

Write your own words:
(look at page 80 for some ideas)

Asking for help

This is hard!
I can't do this!
I don't understand!

Look for an adult to help.

Say the adult's name. The adult
will not know why you have said
their name.

Say: I need help.

Listen to the adult. Wait for the
adult to come to you
or to say: Yes?

Say what you find hard to do.

Private words and public words

Private or personal words...	Instead I can try to say...

A plan to interrupt

Interrupting

I have something to say.
I want to tell my Mum.

I look for Mum.

A plan to interrupt (continued)

My Mum is standing with somebody else.

Listen...

My Mum is talking.

The person is talking.

What do I do?

A plan to interrupt (continued)

I say  Mum

I don't say any more.

I wait: I stand still. I am quiet.

I breathe and blow.

Mum shows me my wait card.

A plan to interrupt (continued)

Mum knows I am waiting.

Mum holds my hand. I wait.

Mum says:

I stop waiting.

I have something to say.

I tell my Mum.

A plan for being told what to do

Sometimes people ask you to do a job.

They might ask:

> Can you get the paper please?

> Ugh!

It's one of *those* sayings where what the person *says* isn't what they actually *mean*.

It's one of those things that by asking it as a question, it sounds more polite. So:

> I want you to get the paper.

> Can you get the paper please?

Sometimes you don't want to do what the person has asked. Sometimes you think the person should have asked more politely. Sometimes parents or teachers ask you to do things. Parents and teachers will *expect* you to do the reasonable things they ask. You may have to try to do the job.

A plan for being told what to do (continued)

☑ Make a plan...

I can think:

> I don't want to do it. I can try to do the job. It will make .... happy.

but say:

> Sure.
>
> No problem.
>
> Okay.

even if I am thinking...

> Yuck!
> Boring!
> Doh!

> Sure.
>
> No problem.
>
> Okay.

A plan for being told what to do (continued)

Even if the adult doesn't say anything, they will probably be thinking something like...

Just because you did the...

Think it, don't say it

I am learning...

Keep practising!

Better and better.

Don't give up.

I did a great job of...

So, do it again!!!

Stop-and-think cards

A plan to sort it out

✐ Calm down

✐ Find an adult to help ◁ I need help to make a plan. Something went wrong.

✐ Meet with the adult to work out what happened...

Draw, write

What happened?

Make a plan for next time

What was hard...? ....

....

....

....

....

....

draw it...

What went wrong...? ....

....

....

....

....

draw it...

Next time my plan will be...? ....

....

....

....

....

....

draw it...

I am amazing!

I can: 🖉

 Yes you can. So go and do it!

Index